Menopaus on th

A Wicked Womans Guide to Growing Old

By Jaki daCosta

Alexis
not totally my sentiments but I'd
love this lady for a pal 'cos
she a fun person   best wishes
Sarah x

CAPALL BANN PUBLISHING

Menopausal Woman on the Run

A Wicked Womans Guide to Growing Old

©1994 Jaki daCosta

ISBN 1 898307 19 9

Cover design & Illustration, by Daryth Bastin, based on a design by Thorn daCosta

Published by:

Capall Bann Publishing
Freshfields
Chieveley
Berks
RG16 8TF

This book is dedicated to a lot of people.

First, my Nan, Beatrice Eele, without whose cups of coffee and Sunday dinners I'd never have got this far.

Next, my son, Thorn, for agreeing to share it with me.

Then Gill, for years of wit and wisdom, Al, for her technical help and emotional support, Shirley for walking up one day and being a friend, Mabelle for being crazy and beautiful, Peggy for hanging in there with our friendship, Johnny for all the years, Jane for being a nice lady with some brilliant kids, Peter, for having the grace to apologize for deflowering me!

Also, Roger and Chad and Andy and Pete, Adam for being a genius, Maude for being an incentive, Evie and Jackie and Paul and Keith.

Jessie and Adam, Lily, Jack, Joe and Ruby and Oceania for being my extended family.

To Nat and Sophie, for teaching me so much.

To Robin and Lizzie.

To Janie......

In short, to all my friends.

And Dusko Sminderovac, for making me find myself.

And to the Goddess, Planet Dustbin, without whose nourishment, none of us would be here!

Jaki daCosta is a writer, performer, witch and rune reader who lives in Hove, Sussex.

Thorn daCosta, her son, is fully house trained, but hates
pigeons. He also lives in Hove.

Contents

GROWING OLD - AND LOVING IT!

Being menopausal doesn't mean
You're suddenly a sexual has-been.
Don't take the word as literal,
Especially if you're clitoral,
And HRT can make you awfully keen!

You save a lot on tampons, that's for sure,
They're really damned expensive, if you're poor!
You know they're taxed as luxuries,
Whereas razor blades are necessities?
I'd love to bleed on Parliament's sexist floor!

I shall miss my monthly bouts of PMTs,
That female psychological disease.
I'd have murder in my bones,
Put it all down to hormones,
And get away with anything I please!

I think I'm going to have a lot of fun,
Now my days of having babies are all done.
All life ends in the grave,
So I'll go out on a rave,
Here comes menopausal woman on the run!

HRT - Hormone Replacement Therapy
PMTs -Pre-Menstrual Tension

We always have choices in this life.

If we can't choose what sex we are, or what talents we are born with, we can choose our attitude to what happens to us.

Growing old is no different.

We may not want it to happen, maybe no-one in their right mind would ask for it, but old we get.

So how are we going to deal with it?

Kicking and screaming, and pouting all the way to the grave?

Or with a cackle, a flourish, a wave of a red-spotted handkerchief as we greet the third stage of our lives like a long lost, long expected friend?

Personally, I go for the second option.

I love growing old.

I think growing old is the nicest thing that ever happened to me.

If I'd known then what I know now. . . . . isn't that how the saying goes?

Well, I didn't. And the past is another country.

At least I've learnt one or two little things along the way of life (roll out the violins!), things I can practise while I've still got breath to enjoy them.

And what I have, above all, is ATTITUDE. In other words, I'm an ageing, ebullient pain in the ass! And I love it!

They say youth is wasted on the young. Too true. Bring all the young to me, let me enjoy them!

Growing old gives me freedom, power and fun.

The freedom to go for what I want, the power to make it happen, the fun of achieving my dreams.

And it's only as we get older that we learn that we evolve with life - it doesn't revolve around us. That's a profound thought from my son, Thorn. Good, huh? I'm not sure I agree with him, but thank God the boy's got a brain!

But, like anything else, growing old only works if you prepare for it properly.

It's no good burying your head in some skin-scouring sand and pretending those aren't wrinkles that are forming, just creases.

What are you going to do?

Iron your face?

The only way to prepare for Old Age is this - look it straight in the eye, wink, and say:

"Hello, sexy. I've been waiting a long time for you. Come and get me while I'm hot!"

Yes, girls, it's strategy or tragedy.

The choice is ours.

GROWING OLD - AND HATING IT!

It's hard being an older woman -
And alive!
A hundred years ago I would be dead
From working in a factory,
Two hundred, from childbirth,
Three - they would have burned me
As a witch!
But this is 1990 plus,
And here I am.
It's hard being an older woman,
Waking up in the morning,
Looking in the mirror.
First the scream,
Then the smelling salts,
Then it's time for positive thinking:
"We have the technology.
We can rebuild!"
Out comes the Rescue Remedy cream,
Then Polyfilla!
It's not so hard
If you're rich and can afford
The operations.
Women like Cher are quite acceptable.
Michael Jackson, alas, poor boy, isn't.
Well, I have tried do-it-yourself
Plastic surgery,
But the pegs keep falling out!
And as for stapling up your tits. . . . !
Forget it!

I've learned to say:
"Oh, don't you know?
They're wearing them slung low
This year!"
Varicose veins can be a problem too.
Well, it gets so wearing,
Always having to make love
With your legs stuck up in the air,
So the blood runs the other way,
And the man you are with can't say:
"Darling, what's that model of the Andes
Doing on your thigh?"
What man?
You may well ask!
It's hard being an older woman
And finding love.
If they're younger than me.
I remind them of their mother.
And if they're older than me,
They remind me of mine!
We frighten people, older women do.
We remind you of decay and death
And all the natural things
You'd rather not remember.
Yes, it's hard being an older woman.
But whoever said life was easy?

It's always been hard, getting old on this planet.

In the past, disease and death took their toll at a much earlier age than they do today.

If you survived into your seventies, you really had earned your soubriquet of "Wise One".

"Lucky One" would also have been appropriate!

However, Sod's Law, that great universal leveller, dictated that no sooner had medical science worked out how to prolong our lives, whether we want it or not - strange world! - than along came the post war economic boom and the focus fell onto the Young Ones - and hasn't shifted away since.

Not fair, huh?

I'm not surprised some people hate getting old.
They're usually the sort of people who believe all the rubbish the advertisers feed us.
The sort of people who believe the world is there to be exploited for our vanity.
The sort of people who believe that death is some sort of horrible mistake, a punishment meted out by a psychotic father.
Psychotic?
Well, would you sacrifice your own son for anything? I should jolly well hope not!

Yourself is the only thing you have a right to sacrifice, and I'd be very careful you don't throw yourself away for an hallucination!

There's no point hating the inevitable.
You're going to end up wrinkled. Fact of life.
Fight it and you just end up wrinkled and ugly.
If you see Beauty only in firm young flesh, you're already going to have a problem adjusting.
If you've got a sour attitude to boot, you're doomed, baby, doomed!

And my Thorn says the flesh is always firmer over there, anyway!

WHATEVER HAPPENED TO THOSE SIXTIES GIRLS?

Whatever happened to those Sixties Girls,
With their Mary Quant make-up and their Vidal curls,
Their Biba dresses and their Kings Road shoes,
Doo waddy music and their boyfriend blues?

Some of us got married,
Some of us just died,
Some of us had babies
And we still survive!

Whatever happened to the Sixties dream,
Love, peace and Woodstock in a world grown clean,
Bob Dylan lyrics round an old camp fire,
Skinning up joints and getting higher and higher?

Some of us got busted,
Some of us got shot,
Some of us turned junkie,
But the rest did not!

Whatever happens now the times have changed,
The Sixties are behind us but the dream remains,
The Cold War's over but the pain goes on,
War and famine and the animals gone?

Some of us are weary,
Some of us are sad,
But some of us keep singing
Cos we're so damn mad!

Yes, it's finally happening to us. The Golden Children, the Flower Power People are having to face their own mortality.

Mick Jagger is no longer the Man Your Parents Would Most Hate You To Marry, but the Grandfather of rock.

The airwaves are filled with old records, each one of which flashes me back to a particular day in my childhood.

And New Right politicians expend a lot of energy on rubbishing the Sixties, trying to blame that era of fun and optimism for all our subsequent ills.

Oh yeah?
Who's kidding who?

The Sixties weren't just a love-in conducted in a haze of marijuana smoke. They were a time of rediscovery of our roots as children of this planet. Herbal medicines, consciousness raising, Save the Whale campaigns, healing all grew out of those balmy days.

Without the Sixties, we'd all be living in a technological concentration camp on a totally devastated world, the victims of greedy and shortsighted opportunists.

And I, for one, concur with the conspiracy theory that the spread of heroin was a direct result of actions undertaken by certain Western governments to destroy the threat presented by free-thinking, virile young men and women. Just as I believe AIDS started in a war-games laboratory.

Of course, there were negative aspects to the sexual revolution that took place. Free love bred lots of babies, and on the whole, it was women who had to carry the responsibility for that.

But if you meet the children of these old hippies, you'll know them instantly. They are articulate, resourceful, caring

ACTUALLY GERALD, WHEN YOU SAID YOU'D FIXED ME UP WITH A 60's GIRL, THIS ISN'T QUITE WHAT I THOUGHT YOU MEANT!

THORN.

individuals. Perhaps their parents didn't manage to change the world in the way they dreamed of, but they changed enough of their own worlds to breed better babies.

That's why it's so important for us oldies to remember that all life is political.

Poverty has returned to the British Isles, not because Joe Bloggs wants £5 a week more in his wage packet, or diddles the dole office for a few quid, but because Thatcher's Children demand millions for playing the Stock Market and megalomaniacs squander other people's money on their own gross ambitions.

And because the new technology doesn't need a work force anymore.

Without a dream of a better society, the one we live in would be unbearable.
We who survived must help keep the dream alive.
We who have experience must help others see the way forward is not through external efforts, but by going within.
Just because we're getting old doesn't mean we can let ourselves drift off into a limbo of nasal sprays and nostalgia.

Time enough for that when we're dead!

A THORN IN MY FLESH

What to do when you're a mother
And the children have grown up?
Seduce some other woman's son,
Or buy yourself a pup?
Take lots of evening classes,
Make up for time you've lost?
I recommend analysis,
If you can afford the cost!
Of course, if you were really smart
You never gave up work,
Just juggled fifty things at once,
And felt you were a jerk!
I think we're meant to fade away
And not give any trouble. . . . .
Well, what I have to say to that is,
Roll on, hubble bubble!
You can get stoned, or take a trip,
Some take to the bottle,
But what I say is,
You're a long time dead,
Why go for it full throttle?
Course, some of us just come back out
And face the world again.
Embarrassing for the children -
I don't think my son came.
So all you fine, young, pretty girls,
With your hormones getting stronger,
Remember, our children are just passing through,
And we live so much longer!

I must admit I never planned to have a baby. Motherhood was so low on my list of priorities that when it happened, I spent the first thirteen years trying to ignore it.

Not smart, huh?

Fortunately, the great roulette wheel in the sky had sent me Thorn. Yes, strange name. His father was (probably still is!) half Norwegian. I wanted to give the little bundle a name to celebrate his heritage. Well, I thought, you can't call a boy Thor, after the god of thunder, not in this day and age. I know, I'll add an 'n' to it! That'll sound better!

We have talked a lot about his conception and birth, my son and I, and I think he's finally forgiven me for loading him with such a psychologically revealing handle! You see, you can heal any mistakes you make in this life, but you have to face them and then give them the time they deserve.

It doesn't matter how old you get, there's always time to talk. Healing occurs when you talk out loud to another person who bears witness.

So my little Thorn has grown into a wonderful big bramble bush, who keeps his mad mother on the straight and narrow. Well, at least when he's around!

14

GOODBYE MOTHERHOOD - PLEASE!

I deserve a happy ending
To the story of my life.
Deserve to know good feelings,
Before they wield the knife!
Deserve the moon and stars to shine,
Deserve to see the sun,
Deserve the best things in the world,
Deserve to have some fun!

Cos I've been mother and wife,
Sister and lover,
Daughter and friend
To one fool or another!
Counsellor, slave,
Audience, star,
Pulling a smile
From a cold cream jar.
All the time
What I really want to be
Is just a good companion
To somebody like me!

I refuse to be supported
In the arms of someone strong,
Refuse to lose the music
Of my rock 'n' roll song.
Refuse the worst a man can give,
Refuse to be ignored.
Refuse to feel what poets feel,

Unless I feel adored!

Cos I've been mother and wife,
Sister and lover,
Daughter and friend
To one fool or another.
Counsellor, slave,
Audience, star,
Pulling a smile
From a cold cream jar.
All the time
What I really want to be,
Is just a good companion
To somebody like me!

Much as I like my little boy... well, extremely big man now, actually... I must say that moving away from that state known as motherhood is one of the greatest benefits of ageing.

Being a mother is awful!

Oh yes, it's all cutesy lovey dovey when they're gurgling little bundles who are totally dependant on you but once they start finding their own feet, you get instantly relegated to a supporting role in someone else's life. Hard to handle, that one, especially, if you were used to having a life of your own.

And you have to get used to things like their rubbishing you, as they develop their independence, their ignoring your well-founded advice as they can't wait to make their own mistakes and their disappearance for months on end as they go off onto courses or whatever, until it's time to come home for a spell of Mum's cooking and laundry duties. And they get so upset if you're not there for them. Always.

17

The little beggars borrow our wombs to come in through, take up all our time and energy for a few years, and then can't wait to rush off into the world leaving us totally unprepared for what we're going to do with the rest of our lives! Bless 'em!

And society is no help here.

Because of the awful psychological conditioning we all live under, which still tries to present motherhood as the only proper aspiration for women, especially Virgin Motherhood (!), a lot of us aren't ready for the third stage of our lives. It's getting better now thanks to Women's Lib. , but even the most liberated woman can get lost behind a bundle of nappies if she isn't careful.

It takes courage to step out into your Cronehood and know there's still work for you to do in the world. I've heard of a bunch of women who refuse to have anything to do with their children once they've grown up. A bit extreme perhaps, but understandable.

Old women have something very important to offer. It's called wisdom and experience. But we have to make ourselves heard and seen.

So don't think you can slip into a mask of invisibility, like a Romulan space ship, just because your mothering is done.
It's time to put on your Hag mask and terrify the bad guys. Much more fun!

YOUR CHILDREN, I BELIEVE. . . . .

In the centre of the circle
Is the centre of the world.
In the centre of the onion
There are tears.
If an onion were the centre
Of the world and all its circles,
Then what we call paranoia
Would be fears.
But an onion is an onion,
And the world's another centre
Like the lotus that is blooming
In my head,
And as fear is but the shadow
Of the giant up the beanstalk,
Then from tomorrow,
Paranoia's dead.

Of course, when you get old, you have two choices in
dealing with other people's children.

One choice is to be an absolute monster and scare the
living daylights out of them. Crude, perhaps, but very
satisfying, especially if you've had enough of your own
children to last you a lifetime.

The other option is to become their adult friend. It's very
important for children to have adult friends.

When we used to live in tribal conditions (ah, halcyon days!), it wasn't the parents who brought the children up. They were too busy hunting and gathering. It was the elders of the tribe who had charge of the juniors' spiritual development, who led them through their rites of passage.

Grandparents should play that sort of part in children's lives, but not everyone today lives near enough to theirs to see them regularly. And there are so many damaged families around, that half the grown ups I know would rather die than have to see their own parents more than once a year at that grimfest we know as Christmas.

So who is to befriend the children?

My friend Gill lets me loose with her mob. I visit, get adored, hear all the secrets the little ones want to keep from Mummy and Daddy and, joy of joys, get to go home again. On my own. Aah, bliss.

You can be totally attentive to other people's children. You can talk to them about life, truth and the cosmos. You can spoil them a little, indulge them a lot and , when it all gets out of hand, you can hand them back to their parents and walk away from the mayhem. Lovely!

I would thoroughly recommend the second option. For one thing, you are giving harassed parents a bit of a break. Ten brownie points for that. You can be a sort of safety valve to the nuclear family. And, believe me, the average family is nuclear. A time bomb, waiting to go off.

It isn't natural for families to live in isolation. Mothers need time for themselves and the support and companionship of other women. Fathers also need space and time to be on their own or with other men. Contemporary marriages seem to be made in a nut house, rather than in Heaven. You can bring a breath of sanity to these bizarre proceedings.

But it's vital you remember never to talk down to the little ones or patronise them. They're too smart for that. They'll see through you like a sheet of Cellophane. Clear and crinkled and discardable.

And you must listen to them, not pretend to. Turn up the hearing aid to full volume if necessary, but listen. If you don't, you'll only add to their confusion and betray their trust, and goodness knows, there's enough people out there in the big world who are going to do that to them soon enough.

Don't be the first.

MUTTON DRESSED AS BIRD OF PARADISE

We are the wicked wrinklies,
And we wear our battles well.
We're limping into life again,
Like visitors from Hell!

And we are here to show you
That it never is too late.
And we are glad to know you,
So, let's celebrate.

Our heads are on our shoulders,
Our feet are on the ground.
And one thing you can say for us,
We sure have been around!

And we are here to show you
That life needn't be a drag.
So pass me up that bottle -
And that strange fag!

Our teeth are in our pockets,
Our gums are at your throat
In case you are a baddy
On this planetary boat.

For we are here to show you
There's a better way to live.
Instead of always taking more,
Learn what you've got to give.

Instead of giving all you've got,
Find out what you should take.
But you'll learn nothing if you sleep
When you should be awake!

So join the wicked wrinklies,
With their one foot in the grave,
Their other on the dance floor
Of their own peculiar rave,

For we are here to show you
That death may always be the end,
But getting there's a bonus
If you head off round the bend!

There's a wonderful poem my friend Peggy sent me a copy of the other day. By Jenny Joseph. About being an old woman and wearing purple. Absolutely. And scarlet. And blue. And pink. And yellow on a dull day.

Colours mean things. It's part of the wisdom to know about colour healing.

Hobbling around looking like an aroused peacock is even better when it's consciously done.

I spent most of my youth swathed in black, like a refugee from a Chekov play.
"Why do you always wear black?"
"I'm in mourning for my life. " Opening lines of 'The Seagull'.

Gothic punks wear black too, but I've never been able to get my hair to stand on end. Too fine. Too thin.

And then, one day, in my late, very late forties, I decided the time had come to wear colour. Now it's scarlet when I am trying to revive a flagging libido, blue when I want to read runes and tell the truth, an orange vest to attract the sun's healing, pink when I want to be friendly as opposed to passionate.

Great Britain is such a grey country, psychically. Not surprising we choose grey men to govern us. The majority of the population seems to want to fade into the concrete, leaving colour and pageantry to the royals. Well, not this girl.

I want to bring colour and fun into people's lives. I want to express all the whims and fantasies that flash into my Sagittarian brain. I want to drape myself in silks, especially now you can buy silk shirts for as little as 9. 99. And I'm lucky enough to live in a town which is rapidly becoming the Charity Shop centre of Europe. You can experiment for pennies so long as you're not hung up on status. And fashion.

Make fashion, don't follow it. Getting old liberates you from having to dress to suit your peer group. Unless, like me, you're lucky enough to have a peer group as crazy as you are!

I'm on a mission to establish the supermarket carrier bag as THE fashion accessory of our time. For one thing, I hate handbags. They remind me of Margaret Thatcher and the Queen and they also encourage mindless young hoodlums to think you've got something worth carrying.

My son may groan, "My mum, the bag lady!", but I know I'm doing my bit for recycling and protecting myself at the same time. Smart thinking, huh, bat person?

For clothes, I recommend soft materials, loose trousers and tops, so you always feel you're caressing yourself, not walking around encased in armour.

And jewellery. Wear lots of jewellry, especially encrusted with crystals and semi-precious stones. Leave diamonds to the rich bitches. They've got precious little else going for them!

I do have qualms about today's version of the big game hunter, the crystal supplier who rips mountains apart to satisfy the "New Age" market's demands for those magical, healing stones. So I practise a "they shall not have died in vain" policy, just as I do with dead animal skins. My flat is festooned with fur rugs and old fox furs, all of which I've picked up for pennies at car boot sales, because I can't bear to think of all those beautiful creatures having been murdered for nothing. But I'd never buy new.

It's the same with crystals.

So, I like to wear rose quartz when I'm trying to remember to be nice to people,amethyst to boost my spiritual aura, amber when I want to crank up my witchy powers and my huge turquoise rings to keep the evil eye away. And if spiritual protection fails, they serve a dual purpose as a knuckleduster! Well, a girl's got to look after herself in this world!

None of my baubles were expensive nor are they particularly valuable, but they are all beautiful. And we need to surround ourselves with beauty whenever we can. It's the antidote to the urban blues.

And when are they going to bring out glitzy, spangled support hose? Do these manufacturers have no imagination?

EXERCISE - BUT ONLY YOUR PREROGATIVE!

Run, jump, skip, hop,
When will this torture ever stop?
Bend, stretch, kick your heels. . .
Does anyone know just how bad this feels?
Why am I putting myself through this?
I must have a streak of the masochist!

My advice to you about exercise is DON'T.

Watching people's grimaces of pain as they pound along pavements, obviously jarring their spine at every step, convinces me that if God had meant us all to run about, we'd have been born with batteries included!

And you can touch your toes ten times easier if you're sitting down!

I keep my tongue in trim and my fingers. That way I can talk and roll fags at the same time. Exercise enough for any woman!

TO BLUE RINSE OR NOT TO RINSE

Hair today but gone tomorrow
Is my son's perpetual sorrow.
Mine is different, it's so thin
It's hard to keep a hair grip in.
Though we sing a different song,
Both of us now wear it long.
Thus we compensate with bulk
For what might otherwise make us sulk!

Untamed hair is erotic. That's why so many monotheistic religions make women cover theirs. The men find it too much of a turn-on! If only the little darlings could control themselves!

I plan to be one of those old women with a long, grey pigtail. I think grey hair's beautiful and natural. And you can always let it down for those special moments!

Voluntarily sitting under one of those heated space helmets strikes me as a bizarre way to spend precious time. And artificially tinting your hair to hide the tell tale signs of ageing usually has the reverse effect and makes older women look ancient!

I admit it's sometimes fun to put some crazy colour onto your hair, though last time I tried it, I ended up with indelible blue fingerprints all over my pink bathroom wall. Ugh! If you want to go blue, go electric blue, that's my advice. Better still, do nothing. Just wash and go. . . . . .

32

THE ONLY THING YOU NEED TO MAKE UP IS YOUR MIND!

Paint and powder can be fun
When you're under forty one.
When you're older have a care,
Or you'll make the fellas stare,
Not because you look so glam,
But cos you're mutton dressed as lamb!

When I was a girl, I wore false eyelashes half way down my face, eye liner to rival Dusty Springfield's and enough eye shadow to cover a Van Gogh canvas!

Not any more!

I admit I'm one of those lucky women who have cheekbones. It's easier facing ageing (pardon my pun!) with those and a good jaw line. Nothing sags. Well, nothing you can see!

Petite, pretty blondes have it all their own way till they're about twenty, but they fade fast.

Us statuesque brunettes - with cheekbones - go sailing majestically on into our twilight years.

So why cover it all up?

I don't want to present a false face to the world any more. The odd bit of eye shadow is about all I can manage these days and then only for parties.

Wrinkles aren't God's health warning against getting old.
They're our badge of pride in the life we've lived. And they
don't come cheap! So if you've got 'em, enjoy 'em. And they
don't get in the way of your love life, either!

SHOPPING CAN BE FUN - IF YOU DON'T DO ANY!

So, Socrates, you were the one,
You little faggot, were you?
Who split us from ourselves,
Putting our minds on pedestals,
Confining all the rest of us
To mechanist oblivion.
Because of you,
The noble savage
To a savage noble
Turned,
And light dimmed from our planet
As the holy women burned.
The rape, the torture
Of our mother earth,
You sanctioned that,
You and your golden boys,
Your pretty toys
Who hung about your intellectual crotch,
Exchanging adulation
For the lecher's touch.
How does it feel now, after all these years,
Do you snug/smug in some Olympian males' only club?
Or are you still turning in an earthly grave,
Wondering why women have shown such scant respect
To someone of your towering intellect?

We live in a material world. Especially us urbanites. If you
don't want to spend money, where do you go in the daytime?
OK museums, cinemas but even they cost. Parks are great, if

it's not p*****g with rain! And even then, it's nice to have a cup of tea somewhere. It all costs.

I hate shopping.
I've never been a good window shopper.
Probably too spoilt when I was a kid.
If I see something I like, I want it then and there. That's why I found having a credit card such a disastrous experience. No self-discipline, you see. I got rid of the card a couple of years ago but I'm still paying off the debt!

And prices! They're outrageous. They're only as high as they are because of credit. If we didn't live now and pay later, retailers would have to keep their prices down so we could afford to save for things.

I've finally managed to wean myself off the shopping drug. The local charity shops are the nearest I get to the big stores nowadays. And you can get everything you need at a car boot sale. Or a market.

Of course, if you want to stay a victim of the Free Market buccaneers, that's your choice. I'd rather stay home and write rude things about them.

And I'm surrounded by so many THINGS anyway, they'll last me two lifetimes!

COOKING,SHMOOKING! WHO NEEDS IT?

When I was young,
I ate a lot
To compensate
For God knows what!
Now I'm old
And have more fun,
I've lost the taste
For cake and bun.
Mounds of food
Do not appeal,
Other pleasures
Seem more real!
And if I never
Cook again,
It will be soon enough,
That's plain!

I hate cooking. Always have! All that preparation and work, and it's gone five minutes later!

I'm not that fond of eating any more, either. I've discovered other appetites through the years!

If only we could eat one big meal a week and live on that for seven days. But no, we have to feed ourselves daily, so I've discovered the perfect recipe. Spaghetti. With tomato sauce. With soya mince. With pesto. With cheese. Whichever way, it doesn't take more than five minutes, and there are only two pans to wash up afterwards.

And cheese on toast makes the perfect breakfast. Only the grill pan needed for that, the way I do it.

However, as a wicked woman, my fundamental diet consists of black coffee and a fag. I've got this wonderful print on my wall, drawn by Paula Cox, of two women, both holding cigarettes, leaning over a pot of tea and talking nineteen to the dozen. It's called Fag Hags. And I'm a founder member of the gang!

I'm very suspicious of all the hysteria directed at smoking these days. To be sure, if manufacturers didn't treat tobacco with umpteen chemicals, it would be safer to smoke regular brands, so I do stick to rolling my own now. But there's so much pollution in the air these days, it seems like shooting at a soft target to accuse smokers of endangering non-smokers' health. I also believe cancer is an emotional disease and if you're prone to it because you're too stressed out all the time, then you're going to get it, smoking or not. Above all, we're all going to die anyway, so I'd rather go with a last puff - and two sugars in my coffee, please. Brown, of course.

By the way, if you do get a smoker's cough - dope is very good for shifting all that phlegm!

All that doesn't mean I don't appreciate being invited out for dinner or lunch. And I'll very grateful for Meals on Wheels when I get too feeble to raise a colander.

And isn't it lucky that men are such good cooks, and love to do it while I'm having another fag and watching them. . . . . ?

P. S. I picked up a saucepan today to boil two eggs in - I love hard-boiled eggs in mayonnaise, even if you had better NOT stand downwind from me after I've eaten them! - and I had to blow the cobwebs off it!

Well, there are no men around at the moment; they're banished while I'm writing.

Good job it's salad season!

WORK IS A FOUR LETTER WORD

If I were an eco-warrior
I'd machinegun the Tories,
I'd burn down their Parliament
And censor their voices.

If I were an eco-warrior
I'd have murdered George Bush.
Don't want to sign the bio-diversity treaty?
There's a cliff.
Here's a push!

If I were an eco-warrior
I'd declare war
On all the multi-nationals
Who are feeding off the poor.

Well, I am an eco-warrior,
But my bullet is my word,
So speak up, all you warriors,
Let your weapons be heard.

There's a narrow line between work and drudgery.

If you're an artist, a musician, a writer, then your work can be your life's mission, and thoroughly enjoyable to be doing that, it is too.

If, on the other hand, you are like the majority of people who somehow got side-tracked into some dreary nine to five

toil that sucks your spirit rather than fires it, then old age is a good time to get back to what you really want to do.

There aren't enough jobs for the young ones these days, let alone a wrinkly. Applying for a regular job can expose you to polite disbelief at the best, downright ridicule at the worst. So why put yourself through it, if you don't have to?

Of course people need money. But old women have power, with or without a chequebook. Some people need to have something to do to keep them alive, but that can be voluntary. And money is only important if you swallow the lies of the Consumer Age. The only thing I've ever done with money is spend it. Poverty inspired me.

And, just as with sex, if you haven't yet explored the talents you always thought you had but never dared to use when you were young, when are you going to do it?

It's never too late to start something new, you know.

You just have to have the will.

DRESSING DOWN

What happened to the Welfare State?
Where did it go at such a rate?
It disappeared at appalling speed
Under the weight of Tory greed.
Jumped up grocers
From humble beginnings
Rose on the back
Of stock market killings
To challenge the fabric
Of our society,
And steal from the poor
With blazing impiety.
They robbed and plundered
The people's wealth
Even putting a price tag
On children's health.
This is what happens
If you educate scum
Well, they're right in that,
Look what they've become!
None of the nouveaux riches
Would have risen
Without the help
Of Socialism.
And so we are living
The nightmare dream
Of a grocer's daughter
Who wished she were queen,
And a B movie actor
Who found his vocation

In ripping apart
The American nation.
What happened to the Welfare State?
It got lost up the a****hole
Of Thatchergate!

Dressing up may be fun, but dressing down is really entertaining, especially when you're dressing down someone who totally deserves it.

Take service. We know nothing about good service in this country.

The English seem to think that everyone should give us their money and not expect anything in return. So much for the market economy. You may laugh at the Americans' "Have a nice day", but I think it makes transactions go with a swing, especially when it's said with a wide smile.

Now that I'm old, I don't have to be nice to anybody who doesn't deserve it. Waiters who bang down plates get an abrasive daCosta comment. Drivers who show no grace get an earful of invective and politicians earn letters to the editor with unfailing regularity. It doesn't matter whether they get printed or not. Some do, but most seem to be libellous. I don't care. It makes me feel good to express my wrath.

Why should I be silent when I see society disintegrating around me?

Why should I swallow the lies spewed out daily on Radio Four? They're probably the same lies spewed out on television, but I try to avoid the one-eyed monster as much as possible. Healthier for the brain.

Villains only stay in power because the majority of the electorate collude with them. Bad service flourishes because too many people take what's given them and only complain to their nearest and dearest. Cowards.

When you're old, you have a duty to speak up. If you can do it with wit, so much the better. After all, I'm old, I don't want to get bashed in the face if I can avoid it. But if we don't teach the youngsters there's a right way of doing things, how will they ever learn?

THE REASON FROGS IS SO POPULAR FUR THE KISSING, GIRLY, IS THAT ALTHOUGH VERY FEW ARE PRINCES, THEY ALL HAVE VERY VERY LONG TONGUES

THORN

SEX - AND HOW TO GET IT

I used to kiss a lot of frogs
While looking for my prince.
The only frog who kissed me back,
I haven't seen him since!

But I believe in fairy stories,
I believe in love and life,
I believe in knights and dragons,
And the fisherman and his wife.

I grew up a Cinderella,
And I suffered like Snow White,
The only difference in our stories
Is that theirs turned out all right!

But I believe in fairy stories,
I believe the good witch wins.
I believe in magic castles
Where the spinning wheel still spins.

One day I'll meet the handsome man
Who loves me for myself,
But with my luck I'll fall asleep
And wake up on the shelf!

I'll still believe in fairy stories,
I'll believe in wishes three,
I'll believe the gods are sleeping
Underneath a magic tree.

Yes, I believe in fairy stories,
I believe in love and life,
I believe in knights and dragons,
And the fisherman and his wife.

The way to get sex is to open your legs, metaphorically speaking.

Love requires a little more finesse.

I think about sex a lot these days. I may not do it, but I think about it. That way I don't get my heart broken, my sheets dirtied or my time taken up with someone else's ego.

But that doesn't mean it's not on offer. It's one of those Sod's Law truths that the less you go looking for something, the more it comes looking for you.

If you're happy with a one night stand, I bet you could get it eight days a week. Boy babies used to die off much quicker than girl babies but good old medical science has changed all that, so now we have herds of unattached men looking for a safe haven for their second heads.

Women have always been more interested in a lasting relationship.

Well, as a Sagittarian, I've never been a great wow in the relationship stakes, myself.

After my umpteenth failure I decided it was time to learn to live with myself since that was obviously what I really needed to do. What a revelation that was! I'm now so contented in my solitary splendour, I can't imagine what it would be like to have some rampant male move in with me.

Or some gorgeous female.

That doesn't mean I don't occasionally try again. It's amazing how many attractive, single people there are out there of all age groups. And there's nothing like getting pissed and stoned to break down my vow of celibacy. But on the whole, I prefer to stay friends with my gentlemen admirers these days and settle for a hug from my lady loves.

We are so narrow in our sexual outlooks. There's only three per cent difference in our genetic make up between male and female, and like everything in nature, that's not an absolute. Of course homosexuality is natural. And what does it matter anyway, as long as sexual relations are conducted with love? Or at least with affection.

There's nothing worse in life than repression. It's unhealthy and damaging. And it leads to projection. You know, when you accuse everyone else of being guilty of what's actually buried in your own mind.

If you can't explore your sexuality as you get older, when can you explore it? And just because you go experimenting among your own kind, doesn't mean you're stepping over some invisible line for ever.

Bisexuality is healthy and probably more common than anyone admits. Come out of those closets before they turn into your coffins. You'll only have to come back and do it all again. Louder.

SEX - AND HOW TO AVOID IT

Women of a certain age
Have a right to feel outrage
When any married male cronies,
Who must look on us girls as ponies,
Want to take us for a ride.
In other words, a bit on the side!
The marriage bed is often thorny,
And men are almost always horny,
So, older women being seen
As desperate, mad, but usually clean,
They think we are the perfect pick
To harbour a frustrated d***!
I hate to have to tell a friend,
He must be round the f****** bend,
If he thinks that I'm so silly
As to accommodate his w****!
No, all my married friends get is talking,
I'll let my fingers do the walking!

Remember the "mercy f***"? It's the name Americans invented for those occasions when some man insists he'll die, or go mad, or be devastated etc. etc. etc. if you don't surrender graciously and give him one.

My advice to you is don't!

As you get older, you'll find those of your contemporaries who are still married, or who are staying together "because of the children" may well try to talk you into some sexual peccadillo. Never fall for it. You may feel you're getting over the hill, that the bluebird of happiness has been shot down over Sarajevo, that if you don't take what's on offer you'll dry up completely or forget how to do it.

Rubbish.

Never give yourself away for less than you're worth. And if you don't think you're worth the best there is, you should be concentrating on sorting that out, not opening yourself up to more punishment.

The best weapon you have to fight unwanted advances with is your tongue. If he comments on your beautiful eyes, tell him they're brown because you're full of s***. If he starts trying to touch you in an overly familiar way, tell him you'll break his arm if he doesn't remove it from around your waist. Tell him you're a born again virgin and you'll only give in to God.

For some reason, a lot of women think they have to submit to advances by men. We don't. When you're hot, you're hot, when you're not, you're not! End of story!

My long, scarlet fingernails are enough to frighten any potential pest away, and I only have to flash them.

And my sense of humour has deflated more tumescent organs than I've had hot dinners!

DO IT YOURSELF SEX

Has anybody here seen my libido?
I know I used to have one,
Now it's gone.
I think I put it somewhere
For safekeeping,
But where I can't recall,
It's been so long!

Well, the other night it happened,
Male presence,
Even got him to accompany me to bed.
But when it came the time
To do the business,
We had coffee and a cigarette
Instead!

Well, it never was a Porsche of a libido,
As sex drives went it only ever had two gears.
The first was, "Do we have to? Oh, alright then. "
The second, "Good, you've come, that's over. Cheers. "

I saw it as a shrivelled little raisin,
Wiped out by years of sexual misuse.
I never thought I'd lose the little bleeder.
My God, to think it's out there,
Running loose!

I bet I find it up the University,
It always went for intellectuals,
It liked head!

Just wait until I get it home to Mamma,
I'll glue it to the bottom of my bed!

So if you notice any alien presence,
Especially you young guys
With long hair,
Don't squash it! It's not lice,
It's my libido,
Just shopping in a
Favourite thoroughfare!

Life's not the same since I lost my libido. ,
Even chocolate has lost its magic taste.
So, girls, if you've still got one,
Better flaunt it.
Don't let a good libido go to waste!

Now I must admit here that you are talking to a woman with a libido lower than the Dead Sea! This obviously makes it easier for me to resist all those lovely men I meet but there's another factor to consider.

Masturbation.

Believe it or not, I'd never heard of it till I was thirty one. I thought it was something public schoolboys did that made their willys fall off. And then I went to America. There, on daytime television, I caught a talk by some learned male on clitoral versus vaginal orgasm. Revolutionised my sex life, didn't it?

Being able to satisfy oneself is extremely useful. Not only does it mean you don't have to go to bed with someone just because you're randy. It also means you can finish off a sexual encounter satisfactorily without you both having to bang away at it all night. Well, an older woman needs her beauty sleep!

And you won't give yourself a sexually transmitted disease, or a baby.

THE IMPORTANCE OF YOUNG MEN WITH LONG HAIR

I wonder if it's age or luck
That makes me the world's
Most indolent f***?
Don't get me wrong,
I can lie there and take it,
So long as my partners
Don't expect me to fake it,
But when it's my turn
To do something physical,
I'm afraid I become
Like a woman invisible.

I think part of the problem is
It's medically true,
That once women climax
Their interest goes too.
That doesn't explain
Why I've got me an attitude
That ranges from boredom
To downright ingratitude.

I suppose that the answer
Lies deep in my past,
In all those relationships
That just didn't last.
The harder I tried
To show my affection,
The faster they ran
In the other direction!

So now, when I screw,
The pleasure's all mine.
They can take it or leave it,
By me, that's just fine.
And I don't even care
If it's age or luck
That makes me the world's
Most indolent f***!

I've always had a soft spot, a very soft spot, for young men with long hair. There's nothing like a "pair of broad shoulders, a toss of long hair" to get my imagination working overtime.

For a start, I find them aesthetically beautiful.

They look like warriors.

Now, a warrior only fights in defence of his home and family, or does battle with the forces of darkness while searching for the Holy Grail. A warrior doesn't have to be aggressive, he leaves that to mercenaries.

For another thing, their beauty is feminine, so they appear to have achieved the balance between the two sides of their nature. Not always true, but a lovely idea for the Aquarian age.

The love of my life was a young man with long hair. Unfortunately, although I was well into my forties when I met him, I was so overwhelmed by his beauty that I promptly turned into ten year old Fatso daCosta on the spot and we never consummated my passion.

Ah well, I live in hope. Or is it Hove?

At the moment, I wouldn't know what to do with one of these little treasures if I had one. Virility can be such hard work! But young men do well with older women, there's so much they can learn from them. And it does a girl's ego a power of good to be seen walking around with some prime time Adonis. Even in friendship.

I might treat myself to a Galahad in a while, when this book's finished. A lot of young men don't want to bring children into the madness this world is descending to, so post-menopausal woman is the perfect companion. And if an entire generation chose not to breed, it would do wonders for the world's over-population problem. So heroic.

At the very least, I see it as my duty to cherish one of these heroes!

THE IMPORTANCE OF YOUNG WOMEN

They banned the Travellers from Glastonbury last year,
They ban them from Stonehenge.
Seems that anybody who works nine to five for a living
Must only want revenge
On anybody wild and free,
Who doesn't play the game.
You think it doesn't matter?
I think it's to our shame.
We've all forgotten how to live, you see,
How to respect the earth.
Forgotten that it's one big round
Of love and birth and death.
Nobody tells the daughters
They're the guardians of life,
And men, you should be warriors,
Not engineers of strife.
The great machine of commerce
Is grinding us to bits.
There'll never be a healthy economy again,
It's got the terminal s****!
They used to call us drop-outs
When we chose not to collude
With ripping off the planet,
Now it's Crusties, sounds more rude!
So don't cheer when the Travellers
Are driven from your gate,
Next year it might just be you,
As refugees of hate,
The hate the nouveaux riches feel

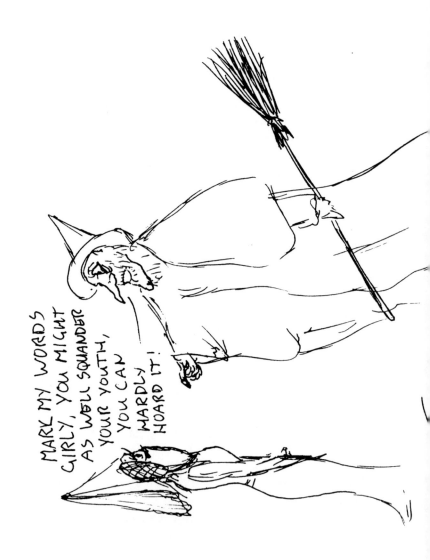

MARK MY WORDS GIRLY, YOU MIGHT AS WELL SQUANDER YOUR YOUTH, YOU CAN HARDLY HOARD IT!

Everytime they see the poor
Asleep in cardboard boxes,
It's a hate could lead to war.
So drink one for the Travellers
Next time you have a few.
Like all endangered species,
The Travellers could be you!

The importance of young women is that they are the mothers of tomorrow and the old women of the day after. Let's help them enjoy their experiences. Pain may be good for the soul, well, some religions say it is, but they seem to be the ones favoured by the masochists and sadists of this world. Unfortunately, damaged parents raise damaged children.

I wish I'd had a daughter. I only ever got broody twice in my life, once when I was 35 and again at 42. Neither time produced a little Rose to match my Thorn.

I had a female dog for several years, but Thorn was never comfortable calling her sister. And I couldn't bring myself to dress her in gingham or put ribbons in her hair!

But I do have surrogate daughters. Girls who've lost their own mothers or are estranged from them. We satisfy some need in each other and I don't have to suffer pangs of jealousy as I watch a little cutie blossom into a stunning swan, eclipsing her Mamma along the way. My fragile ego would have found that very hard to handle at certain times along the way!

No, this way is ideal and it keeps me in touch with The Younger Generations!

I WANT TO BE A WICKED OLD WOMAN WHEN I GROW UP!

What is a witch,
But a woman
Who knows her own
Power,
Reading the feelings
In her guts,
In preference to
The rubbish in
The press?

What is a witch,
But a wild woman,
Raging in fury
At all the destruction
The fools and
The greedy ones
Have wrought on
Our planet?

What is a witch,
But a free woman,
Riding the broomstick
Of delight,
Soaring phoenix-like
Out of the ashes
Of her sisters'
Sad history?

66

This book is described as a wicked woman's guide to growing old. So what is a wicked woman? And why is wickedness something to be admired? Well, let's look at a standard dictionary definition of 'wicked'. This one comes from The Concise Oxford:

"1. sinful, iniquitous, given to or involving immorality. " [heavy stuff, huh? And who defines morality, I'd like to know.]

"2. spiteful, ill-tempered; intending or intended to give pain. " [Well, I agree, that's not nice.]

"3. Playfully malicious." [that's more like it]

And the root?

"Middle English feminine [of course. It had to be!] obsolete 'wick' (perhaps adjectival use of Old English 'Wicca' wizard)."

Or 'witch', as any good pagan would recognise.

Because that's what wickedness is meant to imply - free, dynamic, female feistiness. A spirit that won't lie quietly under her mate and do what she's told. The sort of woman they burned nine million of in The Burning Times. The sort of woman they always label "witch". The sort of woman who's reappearing with a vengeance.

Wipe away that conditioned picture of a witch as a malicious old woman with a wart on her nose, a pointed hat and a broomstick. I , for one, haven't got a wart. Or a pointed hat. And the broomstick is perfect for yard clearing.

Replace it with one of an intelligent, knowledgeable, compassionate woman who believes she is in control of her own destiny. One who believes God/Goddess is in all living things and not just cathedrals. One who believes her will is divine. And effective. Above all, one who thinks for herself. That's why witches were so dangerous to the newly emerging male oriented church and professional classes during the Renaissance. They were the spiritual heart of the people, the healers, the midwives and the funeral directors. They could interpret natural law. Beneath the veneer of Christianity beat a pagan heart and the witches were its voice. So they had to go.

But we're coming back.

Science has failed us. Reason has failed us. Divinity in the sky has failed us. The Earth is calling again for witches and warriors and shamans to defend her.

> To be wicked is to dance to an old, old tune.
> To be wicked is to be a Hag, a holy woman.
> To be wicked is to be a Crone, one who births the living and buries the dead.
> To be wicked is to forget you ever identified with Eve, and remember you were Lilith.

P. S. Just because this is addressed to women doesn't mean there aren't some very good men around nowadays. I love a man with a well-developed anima! Don't you?

THE LILITH FACTOR

My name is Lilith.
I am a daughter of the Goddess.
I am ice, I am fire,
I am life itself.

My name is Lilith.
My home it is the Garden.
I am earth, I am air,
I am free.

Remember me,
All you have forgotten,
Learn my name,
You who never knew.

For I am Lilith,
And this is the Garden,
And I am home again!

So who was Lilith?

Well, according to the Cabbalah - the esoteric book of Judaism, the one where all the heavy stuff that can be used for magick is to be found - she was the first wife of Adam, created free and equal to him, moulded from the earth.

Then one day Jehovah told her that the times they were a'changing and she had to accept Adam as her lord and master and agree to lie under him in the missionary position

WELL ADAM, I WOULD LIKE TO
HELP YOU START THE HUMAN RACE
ONLY YOU'RE STILL MARRIED TO LILITH, AND
I WAS MADE TO BE A NICE GIRL. SO
CAN'T WE FORGET ABOUT
SEX AND JUST
EAT AN
APPLE
INSTEAD?

and stop getting on top as she was used to doing.

Being a spirited woman, Lilith told God exactly what she thought of him and flew out of the Garden to make her home under the Red Sea. From there she flies out at night, causing men to have wet dreams and occasionally carrying off new born babies.

She still enjoys sex but now she 'copulates with demons' and gives birth to countless incubi and succubi, or little devils to you and me. Psychologically, she still yearns for her Adam, her brother/lover and he for her. How could a second rate substitute like Eve ever replace such a dynamic woman in his heart?

This is the true tragedy of the Fall. The Self divided from its Self.

But Lilith often lives again in older women. It's a known fact that once a woman has finished building her career or her family, she may well fall madly in love with some man "as beautiful as Adam" and take the lead in an erotic affair. It's what happened to me, except I didn't manage the erotic bit. Better luck next time.

But why wait till you're old? Helping the young re-integrate Lilith is a vital job for older women.

The Eve myth has been used for centuries to disempower the female spirit. Enough is enough, already. If all the girls get angry enough about what's happening to society and the environment, maybe we'll all finally rise up, kick ass and DO SOMETHING ABOUT IT!

But remember, Lilith sacrificed her love rather than betray her integrity.

It's her independent spirit we need so badly now, not just her horniness.

LAUGHTER IS A GIRL'S BEST FRIEND!

With a hackle, a cackle,
I'll laugh your house down.
I'll prick your pretensions
And knock off your crown.
With a higgle, a giggle,
I'll puncture your puff,
I'll pierce your pomposity
And tickle your tough!
Why won't I stay silent,
Why won't I play dead?
There's too much to challenge,
Too much to be said.
So be warned and beware,
There's a hag on your tail,
And if you don't watch it,
She'll laugh you to jail!

"Oh, my God, Mother," sighs my long-suffering offspring, "That laugh!" Sorry son. There's a lot to laugh about in this life. And to laugh at.

Humour is the ultimate weapon. And the ultimate cure.

I suggest all you sister hags take time out to develop your cackles.

For one thing, it's a great ice-breaker. It's hard to ignore a whooping gale of laughter, and I love to see people shocked

74

into smiling on the street or in cafes. If I can spread a little sunshine as I pass. . . . . . Sunshine? With my laugh it's more like being staked-out at high noon in the desert!

But I cannot stay silent in the face of hypocrisy. Or collude with the self-deceiver. And wit always cracks me up with delight. Why not let it out?

I didn't send off mail-order for my laugh, or take lessons in it. It just sort of developed, the older I got. So I see it as a gift from the Goddess, a way of sublimating my rage at the injustices of life. Gosh, how pretentious! Think I'll laugh at myself for that. I deserve it!

I REMEMBER. . . . WHAT?

Inside my head
I live rent free.
So do twenty others.
I wonder which is me!

Short-term memory loss is a condition shared by dope smokers and wrinklies.

But it's only the day to day minutiae of life that seems to slip out of the brain cells, like a spent condom. Important things like ideas don't disappear. And aren't those what our brains should be full of anyway, not shopping lists?

I thoroughly recommend writing down lists as memory aids. I don't know how I survived so many years without discovering their importance. Perhaps that's why I left it so late to start on my life's work. I don't want my mind cluttered up with "things I must do today". Standing in a supermarket aisle desperately trying to remember what I came in for is not my idea of a fun day out.

I think it's part of a great plot by The System to deflect our attention from the serious issues of life by encouraging us to waste our precious moments racking our brains for. . . . . what?

I've forgotten. Couldn't have been worth remembering, anyway!

WELCOME TO MY SNAIL SANCTUARY

I owe the bank so much money,
It's taken my soul.
My mortgage is busted,
My rock's lost its roll.

But I'm singing, I'm singing,
I'm laughing at the rain.
I'm singing, I'm singing,
Let the music drown the pain.

I bought my groceries on credit,
Now the company's got my card.
I think dying must be easy,
Cos living's so hard.

But I'm singing, I'm singing,
I'm howling at the moon.
I'm singing, I'm singing,
Good times must come soon.

I didn't choose this government,
But it's got me just the same.
Better find me a hole to hide
In a street with no name,

Where I'll be singing, I'll be singing,
They won't kill my song.
I'll be singing, I'll be singing.
Till my ship sails along.

It's good to have a hobby when you get to my age. But you have to be careful not to overdo it.

Gardening's a popular pastime, but the day comes when it's just too much like hard work and not nearly enough like pleasure.

My solution has been to turn the garden over to the snails and practise communing with the little sweeties instead of trying to wipe them out. So much more holistic.

Have you ever practised talking to animals?

Don't laugh. I'm not crazy. I've had a couple of memorable experiences with wild animals. One was a country rat who got trapped in a cottage I was staying in. The cats were after her (I'll call it 'her' for the sake of argument. I didn't actually look to see!), so I decided I had to rescue her.

First I took her to the field outside the gate, but she seemed fazed by the expanse of it. I picked her up again and took her to a nearby cottage's garden, but she obviously didn't like the look of that and refused to leave my side. Finally, I deduced that she must have come from the field behind the cottage, so I carried her there. She ran to the edge of the field, ran back and back to the edge again. She seemed all excited. At last, she ran back to me, scampered up my arm and kissed me on the cheek. No kidding. Then she raced off and

I never saw her again.

My other experience was with a big rook that fell exhausted at my feet during a rain storm. I picked him up (yes, we'll call it 'him' this time. Something about that glowering eye seemed very masculine!) and held him while he recovered his breath. The rain was so heavy that I decided we would be better off sitting in my car. By this time I was developing a fantasy of having this beautiful bird come live with me. Maybe sit on my shoulder like Long John Silver's parrot. I think he read my mind. Because no sooner had I driven to my house and got him out of the car than he managed to fly off and take refuge in a nearby tree.

I learnt my lesson there. Wild creatures are wild creatures. They may share a little of their time with you, but they can never belong to you.

Bit like people, really.

I tell you these stories to show what interesting things you can get into, as long as you have an open mind. What other hobbies can you take up?

I've begun making rune sets. A little carving, a little polish, a little sewing of a suitable bag and hey presto! another pleasant evening passed creatively. Making music is a good hobby. A guitar's not very heavy and singing is a great way to bring people together. Writing is excellent. A pencil is very light and if even I can master a word processor (bought second hand), anybody can. I'm not a very competent artist, but I discovered the joys of stencilling. Now my flat looks like a stage set and I can always tart up a bit of old furniture for a friend.

People have such fascinating hobbies. My old friend, Johnny is a pole lather. That's a primitive wood turner, although there's nothing primitive about the chairs he turns out. Roger was an actor who keeps his hand in with the local amateur company. I met Lavender, a wonderful woman in her seventies, on a workshop that involved absailing and rock climbing.

I don't think she subsequently took it up as a full time hobby, but at least she gave it her best shot once!

Want to try sky diving? Give it a go. You may do an Icarus but at least you'll have something to talk about next time you drop into a seance!

MEDICATION V. DRUGS

When you're young and smoking dope,
You often fall asleep.
Getting out of it, it's called,
As if we all were sheep.

But dope can open up your mind
And let you breathe with trees,
Reveal the mystery of life,
And help you ride the breeze.

And smoking dope's political,
Make no mistake in that.
It separates the shaman
From the greedy plutocrat.

It frees your thoughts,
And helps you fight
That bitch, Conditioning,
The trick that keeps us victims
Of the Church, the State, the King.

So skin up, girls, or light a pipe.
Get into it, I say.
Too old for sex I may well get,
But not too told to play!

The main thing to remember about medication is not to take any!

There has been more damage done by prescribed drugs such as Valium than has ever occurred through smoking any form of marijuana I've ever heard of. And I've heard of a few!

Medication is dished out to old people to keep them quiet and malleable. Well, I have no intention of keeping quiet. And I'm not going to have anybody handling me, thank you very much!

Even that latest top of the pops for menopausal women, Hormone Replacement Therapy, is derived from horse urine! And nobody seems remotely concerned that we might all start whinnying and pawing the ground one day! Perhaps they assume all us old girls are so desperate, we'll take anything. No reason for manufacturers to think otherwise, considering how we've allowed Consumerism to swallow us all up. But that's another story. . . .

Of course there's a place for legal drugs - if you have an accident or an infection - but they are few and far between.

Sensible people get into herbal medicine and part of the traditional wisdom of the Crone was her knowledge of herbs and how to administer them. Today it's called 'alternative medicine' and is easily available through health food shops and mystic shops and healing centres. We don't have to go out at midnight under the full moon with our hot little sickles clutched in our arthritic old hands any more. Not unless we want to! And there's a whole array of books to teach us what we need to know, or therapists and healers, if we can afford them, or terribly helpful shop assistants, if we only bother to ask.

There's no need to be a victim all your life to the mysteries of medicine. Doctors do their best, but a lot of them are too overworked to have much time for a chat and are trained only to set bones and administer chemical drugs. A slight overstatement, I admit, but only slight. And don't talk to me about genetic research! That's Devil's work, if ever I've heard of any!

We have to learn to heal ourselves. And if that doesn't work, then turn for help to someone on the same wavelength.

Now what the law incorrectly labels "soft drugs" and makes illegal is another ballgame altogether.

I call them the planet's gift to consciousness-raising - me and Bill Hicks, that wonderful, late American comedian. And to what are both referring? Marijuana and magic mushrooms, of course.

Throughout history these have been used as herbal medicine and to experience religious visions. It's quicker than fasting and just as effective! There's even a peyote church somewhere in the USA, but I don't think they'll let me join, even if I swear I'm a bona fide Christian! South American Indians used to save some of their coca leaves for the old folks to chew before the Spaniards and the Mafia got their hands on the cocaine business and ruined it and what better to give to an aged Chinaman than a nice pipe of opium to while away his time with?

Sweet dreams!

It's a fact that most of the greatest English poetry of the nineteenth century was written under the influence of opium. And many a Victorian baby was lulled to sleep with a nice spoonful of laudanum, which I believe was a preparation of opium soaked in brandy. That would put a smile on a Christmas pudding!

MEDICATION V. DRUGS, I HAVEN'T GOT ANY ANSWERS BUT IT WAS ONE HELL-OF- -A CONTEST!

The problem with these 'drugs' is not that they're illegal. That's an inconvenience, not a problem. The problem is that there are too few competent guides around today to lead us through the labyrinths of our minds. And taking them alone, or in a social situation, can lead you into paranoia or Breughel's Hell.

Of course, with perseverance, you'd work through those stages, especially with a little counselling or analysis on the way! But it's a dangerous path to travel alone.

It's perhaps fortunate that opium is rarely available in this country these days. It can be addictive if you've got that sort of personality and certainly it's manufactured derivative, heroin, causes nothing but grief and should be avoided at all costs. Likewise crack, derived from cocaine. But a little of the real thing. . . . . . ?

When you're old, what have you got to lose?

A lifetime's prejudices?

For a pleasant evening's dreaming, or a fascinating conversation with a few good friends, I can recommend nothing better than a nice pipe of hashish. Or a joint, if you're a fag hag, like someone I know not a million miles from here!

For those not in the know, hashish is made from the oil of the marijuana plant. Where the leaves can make you giggly, the oil can make you visionary. Decisions. Decisions! What shall I try tonight?

Neither is addictive, nor does regular use lead on to dabbling in harder drugs. That's an urban myth. If you want to go to Hell, you may take the scenic route. If you want to

"I DIDN'T EVEN KNOW MINE HAD GONE MISSING!"

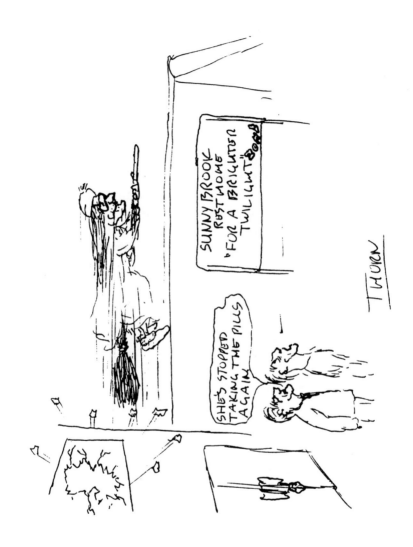

87

stay in Heaven, nothing's going to drag you out of it! And for old people, in particular, the therapeutic, pain-killing benefits of marijuana are incomparable. Queen Victoria used it, for goodness sake! There's no hangover and they won't bring out the aggression in you. Unlike Britain's most popular legal "drug", alcohol, which can turn a mild mannered Clark Kent into the Incredible Hulk, and ruin your liver into the bargain! Not a lot of choice there, I fancy!

No, you would be well advised to budget for a little bit of dope out of your weekly pension. It'll be money well spent, especially if among your gang of grinning geriatrics you can count the neighbourhood dope dealer as one of your long time friends!

Or it's one of the treats you can get the kids to bring you on their weekly visit to Stalag Geriatrica, otherwise known as The Old Folk's Home! I bet you bought them enough sweeties when they were the helpless ones!

THE SINGLE WRINKLY

Sex is a search for a lost mother's titty!
I don't get the sex, so I write me a ditty.
I sing out my frustration, I love through my song,
One day I'll discover where it is I belong!

In the meantime, in between time,
I'm singing.
In the meantime, in between time,
I'm winging!

A pair of broad shoulders, a toss of long hair,
A twinkle of blue eyes, and I think I'm there.
A swing of his hip, a shake of his leg,
And I'm almost ready to crawl, steal or beg!

In the meantime, in between time,
I'm singing.
In the meantime, in between time,
I'm winging. !

I don't have a lover, but I've got lots of friends,
My life is a story of beginnings and ends,
But I'm out there looking, I'll never give in,
Cos in my religion, sex is no sin!

In the meantime, in between time,
I'm singing,
In the meantime, in between time,
I'm winging!

Don't ever be afraid if you find yourself living alone in your old age. With a little bit of organisation and networking you can cover yourself in case of emergencies, leaving yourself lots of lovely time to spend on ALL THE THINGS YOU EVER WANTED TO DO.

Make sure you have a double bed. My friend Peggy says no woman over forty should ever sleep in a single bed. For one thing, you never know when you might want company! For another, you deserve the luxury of sleeping in as much space as you want. And you don't have to be embarrassed if it gets windier under the bedclothes than it is outside the window! There's room on the surface for notebooks and novels and nail polish and address books. And somewhere for visitors to sit, if they're cute enough to be allowed into your inner sanctum.

My bed doubles as a desk. My table doubles as a desk. My desk doubles as a desk! And my floor has its piles of papers and whatnots, too.

You can't live like that if you've got to share your space with someone else. I can't imagine now, having to consider another person's feelings or needs or wants. Male or female. Not in MY flat. If you live in a place big enough for you to have a room each plus one more you can share, then it's probably alright to pool resources with a mate or a pal. After all, the upper classes have been living that way for years! But if, like me, you've got one bedroom and one living room only, better to keep would-be immigrants away.

There's always a spare bed for the odd stay over, but like other people's children, the nicest thing about visitors is that sooner or later, they go home!

Then your time is your own again.

What to do with it?

Well, I'm sure everybody's got their own pet pastime, but for me, the greatest joy is doing rituals. I'm one of those old witches who like to work alone, you see. There's a lot of us around. Coven meetings can be fun, and your fellow witches very sweet, but for real power and focus, there's nothing like pulling the curtains tight, lighting the ritual candles, creating sacred space - and getting down to business.

But do remember not to burn the place down in the process! Firemen may be sweethearts and you may find uniforms a turn on, but you feel such a fool if you wished hard for money and it comes in the shape of a devastated home and an insurance settlement!

A GIGGLE OF GERIATRICS

A woman's place is in the home,
That's what the buggers say,
And if you try to get outside,
They really make you pay.
There's lower wages,
Bottoms pinched,
Promotions for the boys.
It makes me long for yesteryear
When we were more than toys.

When women ruled the world,
When women ruled the world,
We didn't fight
To prove our might,
When women ruled the world.
When women ruled the world,
When women ruled the world,
We lived in peace
With man and beast,
When women ruled the world.

A woman's work is never done,
Although it's limited
To washing nappies, cooking chips,
Consoling dear old Fred.
We long to show our power again,
Regain our rightful place
As leaders of the universe,
Not just a pretty face!

When women ruled the world,
When women ruled the world,
We invented law
And so much more,
When women ruled the world.
When women ruled the world,
When women ruled the world,
The men all knew
Who was number two
When women ruled the world!

And now our time has come again
When we must all awake,
Not from some handsome prince's kiss,
Who wants our power to take,
But from a sense of urgency
That time is running out
To save this little world of ours -
And that's what it's about.

When women rule the world,
When women rule the world,
We'll bring down light
The dark to fight,
When women rule the world.
When women rule the world,
When women rule the world,
We'll never kill
Just for the thrill,
When women rule the world.

Tomorrow is another day,
Another chance to strive,
Unless the buggers all decide
They don't want us alive.
But if they drop a bomb on us,

Our ghosts will still march on,
And through the nuclear winter time
Will echo still our song:

If women ruled the world,
If women ruled the world,
You wouldn't be dead,
You'd survive instead,
If women ruled the world.

When women rule the world,
When women rule the world,
We'll never cruise
In Maggie's shoes,
When women rule the world!

Sometimes there's no alternative for a Golden Oldie than to move into the Old Folk's Home.

I suppose how well we survive this experience depends on how many of our wits we've got about us when we arrive. This is when you'll be glad you've learned to avoid medication. You can always spit out their pills and replace them with a tab of acid, if you find reality too grim!

But there's definitely a positive side to living in a group. Strength in numbers! There's no knowing what a bunch of wicked old wrinklies can get up to, if they only set their minds to it.

Your chief asset, girls, is charm. Charm will wrap anybody round your little finger, even if that finger is arthritic these days. Bribery's good too, but more expensive! Try and get some of the staff on your side. That way you'll always have someone to run errands, or bring in supplies.

There's lots of lovely young men and women doing Community Service or Care Work these days. Remember they're our friends.

So what do you want to achieve, with your band of fellow conspirators? Supplying Animal Liberationists with Kalashnikov rifles? Making bombs for Greenpeace? The sky's the limit, girls, as long as you're working for the light!

And today's freedom fighter always becomes tomorrow's terrorist. Remember when the IRA were heros? I'd rather be known as The Toothless Terrorist than be accused of colluding with the System. Better still, just call me a Warrior of the Rainbow.

And if anybody in the home tries to give you a hard time or mistreat you, tell them you'll turn them into a toad. Or set your son on them, if you're lucky enough to have one!

GOT THOSE PUBLIC TRANSPORT, CAN'T GET ON AND OFF THE DAMN BUS BLUES!

I'm waiting for a bus that never comes.
Listening for a tune that's never hummed.
And I'm walking out of paradise alone,
What good is paradise on your own?

I'm smiling with a smile that isn't true,
Talking to a man who isn't you.
And I'm walking out of Paradise alone.
What good is Paradise on your own?

The colours of the rainbow
Have turned to black and grey,
The little bird of happiness
Has flown the other way.
If I'd known then what I know now,
I'd have known the things to say
To stop you, when you let me
Walk away.

So I'm calling on a phoneline that is dead,
Talking to a love that's in my head,
And I'm walking out of Paradise alone.
What good is Paradise on your own?

The day your legs start giving out is the day you are reminded of the imperfections of the public transport system.

Although I'm lucky enough to have my own transport, only a crazy woman would drive her car downtown where I live. Driving it's OK, it's parking that's impossible. And since the buses introduced a 50p flat fare to cover the exact area I need to travel, just as I really began to need them, I've joined the struggling young mothers and my fellow old feeblies on the number 5.

Watching the former perform feats to rival Houdini's in folding and unfolding those clever little pushchairs, while trying to prevent their offspring from slipping off outrageously high steps, reminds me how lucky I am that those days are behind me.

Then I watch very old ladies struggle to load those four wheeled shopping trolleys into spaces not designed for them while searching for their change under sharp edged ticket machines and I clutch my plastic carrier tighter, vowing never to give into the dreaded shopping trolley while I have breath in my body.

My advice to you on public transport is use it, if you have to, but take your mountaineering gear with you! And I won't even mention trains. A train may take the strain, but it'll take a good portion of your pension as well!

WANNA RIDE IN MY VOLVO, LITTLE MAN?

I was sitting in a waddy, singing doo waddy dan,
When a shadow fell, it was a travelling man.
"Hey, gorgeous, what'd be your name?
Is this your first time visit?
Aren't you really glad you came?"

Oh Mamma,
Tell me what to do!
I'm feeling kinda insecure
When I look into his eyes so blue.

I told him I was busy, didn't want to fall in love.
He fixed me with his roving eye, put on his velvet glove,
Said, "Don't be afraid, I'm not a wolf ,I've a hairy coat,
Not a cloven hoof!"

Oh, Mamma,
Take this little girl home.
She's falling for a travelling man
With a toothbrush and a comb.

He touched my hand, I fell apart,
Then this travelling man rode off with my heart.
Said, "Grow up time. You're very sweet,
But I'm just a man with an itch
In my feet. "

Oh Mamma, you didn't raise a fool,
But a girl's no chance
When she catches a glance
From a man with an itch in his tool!

Boudicca couldn't have felt more protected in her war chariot than I do in my ancient Volvo. It's the nearest thing to a tank I know. Nobody messes with a Volvo! Parking is a problem, though, because it feels about twenty feet long and I do seem to touch a lot of bumpers these days! Why do men get so upset when you back into their precious bumpers? I thought that's what they were made for!

I don't intend to be one of those truly antique drivers you too often find meandering down the middle of the road in my town - a car is a potentially lethal weapon. And who can afford the fines, anyway?

But while I've still got a brain cell or two functioning and the right glasses to correct my deteriorating sight, I still get a thrill from a spin in the countryside, stereo blaring rock 'n' roll as loud as it'll go on only three speakers, window down, fag in mouth, doing all of forty miles an hour on the open road! Makes me feel like a refugee from a road movie. Not very Green, I know, but it's great for giving people lifts!

Because I'll never be a yuppie and cars are so expensive to run now if you're not, I do a car share with my friend, John. Suits both our purposes and keeps one extra car off the road. And cars are great for driving home the cutest young man from the party! Tee Hee!

THAT'S NOT A BROOMSTICK -
THAT'S MY BICYCLE!

This is the Dreaming Time.
Change the dream.
This is the Dreaming Time.
Live it!

On a summer's day - remember those? - there is nothing nicer than climbing on a bicycle and freewheeling off down to the sea front. I'm lucky where I live - it's flat all the way!

You don't have to try to prove you could still do the Tour de France. And for Heaven's sake stay away from those ghastly, hi-tech cycling shorts that look like designer incontinence knickers! No, a gentle pedal is quite sufficient, a lazy weave among the pedestrians. Pedestrians?

I forgot to mention, NEVER go on the road, it's far too dangerous. You may get shouted at by the occasional Tory pensioner, but at one mile an hour I'm hardly presenting a threat to their life and limb. And as a car driver, I know just how irritating it is when some holistic pedaller insists on claiming their right of way on a road choc a block with heavy traffic.

Yes, cycling is much healthier and kinder on the environment. And yes, every road should have a cycle lane. But they don't. And if it comes to a contest between half a ton of solid metal and a bicycle frame. . . . well, there's NO contest.

My sense of self-preservation ranks infinitely higher than my respect for the law. Nor do I see why I should have to deny myself any pleasure just because it might cause a minor inconvenience to some other miserable old fart!

With the wind in my hair and the sun on my face I'm as happy as Don Quixote, looking for windmills to tilt at.

And who knows, one may just fall over!

100 THINGS TO DO WITH A ZIMMER FRAME

There are blue flowers at my feet,
And half the trees are in blossom,
And half are not.
And I have one foot in
The New Age,
And one foot not.
But all my soul is,
So,
Soon I will rise, limping,
And join you there.

The thing to do with geriatric aids is accept all they offer you. You never know when they might come in useful. You don't have to use them as suggested, but with a little imagination, they can serve to decorate your life. And you'll have them if you need them.

Zimmer frames make great little clothes horses, or substitute tent frames when the children come to call. With a bit of wire mesh added, they are great fire guards, if you're a gas fire woman, like me. And excellent clothes rails if you've too many shirts to fit into the wardrobe.

Bed pans are a whizz as flower pots. Or bird baths.

Trusses can be brightened up with a bit of decorative paint work and used as a substitute cod piece, if you want something to wear at a bondage party. And wheel chairs. . . .

ah bliss! I've never got over a past life where I got spoiled being carried around in a litter by four hunky men (mmmmmm! Those litter bearers!), so with a bit of eyelash fluttering, a mobile chair is a great way to pick up young Adonises. "Could you just get me over this road, young man?"

A stick with a detachable head is very useful too. You can always keep your dope in it and it's the perfect tool for tripping up idiots who irritate you. Nobody said you had to turn the other cheek. Not in my philosophy!

WANNA GO TO A PARTY?

Only today the door bell rang,
And oh, how my life changed!
Nothing from this moment on,
Will ever be the same!

And oh, how I love to dance,
Love to feel my feet.
Oh, what a fine romance,
Dancing down the street!

Only today, when you saw me smile
And recognised my soul,
I knew I'd never have to die,
Or lose my rock 'n' roll.

And oh, how I love to dance,
Love to feel my feet.
And oh, what a fine romance,
Dancing down the street!

Who knows where the road will lead,
Or who the bombs will hit.
As long as we're all dancing,
Do you really give a s***?

And oh, how I love to dance,
Love to feel my feet,
And oh, what a fine romance,
Dancing down the street!

You're never too old to party! That's what I say. You don't have to get drunk as a skunk or make a complete fool of yourself trying to outshine all the nubile young things, but you get to talk to some new people and a safe place to dance in.

I don't think the English really know how to party. I despair seeing young men sitting like blocks of wood as the music whips up a rythmn. Or gorgeous girls shyly refusing to be the first on the dance floor. Too many inhibitions those Anglo-Saxons have.

If no-one's invited you to a party recently, you can always throw one yourself. But that's hard work and a lot of responsibility. Better to make it known among your young acquaintanceship that you're getting into party mood and want to be invited somewhere. That usually does the trick. People like having switched on oldies at their parties - we've had years of practice in how to have a good time!

But don't go to one if all you're going to do is tut tut and create a 'them and us' ageist barrier. Nobody needs that - least of all you!

WANNA COME TO MY FUNERAL?

If I should die tomorrow,
Think only this of me -
That I felt love, and I felt pain,
I felt the sun and I felt the rain,
I was burned in the fire
Of life.

If I don't wake in the morning,
Don't waste a tear for me.
Cry for my song,
Cry for me gone,
Cry cos you miss me
And nobody's here long.
But don't cry
Because you think
That I should have seen a shrink
And assigned myself a
A cross
Of humility!

If you should read this poem,
Or listen to my tune,
I hope it makes you feel
You've got s*** stuck to your heel,
If you don't go howling,
Or won't go howling,
Or don't know about
Howling
At the moon.

It's never too early to plan your own funeral. My friend Al is 32 and already knows exactly what she wants. She's going gift-wrapped. In yellow paper. "Because God is getting a hell of a present!" Absolutely! I'll drink to that!

We have to get rid of this taboo we've developed about death. Death is a natural part of life. But the way we go on in our society, you'd think it only happened to other people. On television.

It wasn't until a wonderful "sister", Evie chose to die at home and so made a present of her death and dying to all of us that I had any direct experience of death. And what a change it made to my life. Now I appreciate living.

Chad, another pal, remembers seeing his Gran laid out when he was a toddler. He's been aware ever since that life is a precious gift we're privileged to enjoy for a limited span. So we might as well make the most of it.

I want to die on a hillside somewhere like the Himalayas and be eaten by a wild animal. Then I'll really feel I'm playing an active part in the cycle of life.

What if I die in Hove? In that case I want a pagan service, celebrating my return to the arms of the Great Mother and a flimsy coffin that'll rot away quickly so that all the minerals and goodies in my flesh and bones can seep back into the soil and help regenerate the spot for something else to grow on. Like a tree.

And if anyone insists on inflicting my rotting bones with a tombstone, I want "One for the road!" inscribed on it, because that's how I intend to go!

If I do die among my family and friends,I want everyone to have a party, of course. That goes without saying. Lots of sex 'n' drugs 'n' rock 'n' roll to give me a great send-off. I might even hover around a while in my spirit form, just to make sure you're all enjoying yourselves. . . . . .

SINGLE TO KATHMANDU, PLEASE!

There are many people in this world
Who share a fantasy
Of living on an island,
In the blue Aegean sea.
Those of them who make it
Seem to have a common bond -
The ability to drink enough
To fill a village pond!
There goes the ex-guitarist,
Whoops! He's fallen off his strings,
And there's the would-be actress,
Who guzzles beer and sings.
Here comes the former engineer.
He's nice, but he has fits!
And there's the local lager lout
And all the other gits!
Poetry? Forget it?
Philosophy? What's that?
Beauty's in a bottle,
And drinking's where it's at.
So, somewhere out in Paradise,
In Homer's fabled land,
Sits a sad, unhappy boozer,
With a bottle in his hand.
That hand may shake, his body fail,
His wits may fall asleep,
But one thing that'll he'll tell you is,
"At least the wine is cheap!"

Holidays are good for you! Take as many as you can! If you can't afford to go up the Himalayas or down the Amazon, take a day off in your own town, go to a part you don't normally visit and sit and write postcards to all your friends!

And don't be afraid to go somewhere on your own. You'll soon meet other people to hang out with. But don't bother with hotels if you're a single.

There's a scandalous surcharge they slap onto people booking into hotels alone. It's called the 'single supplement'. The excuse is that hotel rooms are designed for couples so they lose money if only one person sleeps in it. Oh yeah? I've offered to share a room with another traveller, but they won't hear of that. They just want your money. So tell them to get lost and go stay in a youth hostel. Much more fun. And infinitely cheaper. And you won't be surrounded by oiks who think going abroad means you find a place as much like home as it could possibly be and to whom travelling implies the journey from the bar to the poolside and back again!

If I'd wanted to be surrounded by idiots, I'd have gone into politics!

STROKE THAT PUSSY!

In the dark hours of the night,
Which sometimes ask for tears,
Sometimes for love or loneliness,
She grappled with my feet.
A soft, small bundle hiding from the moon,
Buried in caverns made up of my bedclothes.
A few short weeks I knew her,
Not really long enough to get acquainted
Beyond acquaintanceship, and yet
I loved her. Wild and brave,
Racing in circles round and round the room
Or scratching out to catch
Whatever hand had fed her -
And yet at night, a gentle, lovely thing,
That curled up close as if in safety,
Warm and loving, as if afraid to be alone.
I was afraid. I needed her.
She was my lover, son, old ghosts departed,
Old sorrows gone. She was my refuge in the dark.
I was alone and she was there.
I cannot think she needed me,
But in those sad, black hours
She gave me company. No questions,
No demands, but she was there.
The Battersea cat gave more
Than any man.
And gave it
Free.

What a miserable young woman I was when I wrote that! But it was a nice cat.

I've got a nice cat living with me at the moment. It came to my door a few months ago and demanded to be let in. I swear she checked out every flat in the street before she found the one with the curtains that match her colouring! Such a tasteful puss!

Although pets are a problem if you want to go a-wandering, they are great companions the rest of the time. Dogs are good at keeping burglars away, but need exercise. A definite drawback. Birds have to live in cages or you'll be wearing interesting decorations on your shoulder a lot of the time. Fish are difficult to stroke.

No, it's no accident that Crones through the ages have been associated with the four-legged feline. Cats are independent, don't eat a lot, love the occasional cuddle and bring you interesting little gifts from the great outdoors. The perfect playmates, really. But they will bring their boyfriends home, sometimes!

Ah well, nobody's purrfect.

Sorry!

LAWS WERE MADE TO BE BROKEN

Law is a conspiracy against the poor.
The rich make 'em, the poor break 'em,
And if we can't scrape up the money for the fine,
We do time.
Law is a weapon of control of the many by the few.
So what's new?
As religion is control of people's minds,
So law their moral choices curbs and binds,
Keeping us all prisoner of Big Daddy in the sky,
Exploited by the greedy whom it suits to sell the lie.
I do not need their laws to tell me what
And what not to do.
Do you?

If you've lived the average, law-abiding life, then isn't old age the time when you can slip off the straightjacket if you want and live a little dangerously?

Who's going to put that sweet little old lady in prison for shop-lifting? Goods are too damn expensive now anyway and a girl deserves a treat once in a while!

And policemen might go easier with their batons if they're faced with a row of outraged Grannies at that political protest meeting.

There are too many laws in this country. I know it's how you run a democracy, but it's also how you control the majority.

Law breaking has always made me feel like Robin Hood. If I can outwit that big institution and get away with it, brilliant. If I get caught, I go into my daffy old lady act and play for sympathy.

But I'd never hurt anybody or take from someone as poor as me. There's no fun in that. And remember the law of return states that what you do returns on you threefold.

Be wicked, not evil.

CREATIVITY V. THE BLOB

You found a woman who could ride you,
Who could put you through your gears.
Bring out the beast inside you,
Wipe away your fears.

She made you a prancer/dancer,
She made you the stuff of life.
She made you a fine romancer.
You made her the dancer's wife!

She got you to your gigs on time,
Made everything run smooth.
Kept you off the beer and wine,
Well, you couldn't handle booze!

You became a prancer/dancer,
You became the stuff of life,
You became a fine romancer,
She became the little wife!

They put your picture everywhere,
They put your name in lights.
Made you the girlies' darling.
Kept her out of sight!

You remained the prancer/dancer,
You remained the stuff of life,
You remained the fine romancer.
She remained the little wife!

One day she found she'd had enough
Of living in your shade.
Nothing ever compensates
For missing the parade!

She became a prancer/dancer,
She became the stuff of life,
She became a fine romancer,
And she didn't need a wife!

If you've spent your whole life hiding your light underneath the bushel of someone else, then isn't now the time to come out of the shade and find out what really ticks inside you?

There are a lot of blobs walking around on this planet. People who don't use their brains, who always have an excuse for not taking risks. They contribute nothing to life. Just take up space.

Wouldn't you rather be one of those alert old duckies, always brewing up some new scheme for making the day go with a swing?

I believe all people have creativity inside them, unless they're totally brain damaged. Call me an optimist, if you like. Thorn says optimism is the disease of the Sixties Girl, but if that's a disease, who wants to get cured?

There are art classes and creativity workshops to attend if you feel a bit rusty. They all do reductions for pensioners and those on low income. Feeding your soul or your spirit is just as important as putting food in your body. As long as you don't want to become a serial killer, that is!!

It's a fact that having interests in life helps you achieve a healthier Cronehood. Because sickness starts in the mind. You did know that, didn't you?

The most powerful tool in a person's life is their imagination. I - magi - nation. I, the magician of my world. Idea. I - dea. I, the goddess. All the clues are there in the language. Trust your instinct and pick up that paint brush. It's more fun than vacuuming!

WHO WANTS TO BE SANE IN THIS WORLD?

What makes a man an a******e to his wife?
What makes a man an a******e to his wife?
Did his mamma never teach him,
Was his poppa never there?
Was there no-one who could reach him,
Pull him back from black despair?
What makes a man an a******e to his wife?

What makes a mother run off from her kids?
What makes a mother run off from her kids?
Was there no-one who could help her,
Give her back-up and support?
Is society so f****d-up,
We can only write reports?
What makes a mother run off from her kids?

What makes a parent beat up on their child?
What makes a parent beat up on their child?
Was there no-one who could save them,
Was there no-one who could see,
That they were really hurting,
And then they were hurting me?
What makes a parent beat up on their child?

What does it take to make a better life?
What does it take to make a better life?
Is there no-one out there learning,
There's a price for being free?
And what we have to pay with

Is responsibility?
That's what it takes to make a better life.

We live in a crazy society. Things have more value than life. A minority lives in luxury at the expense of the majority. And multi-nationals devastate the Third World for the sake of their shareholders' dividends. And this is considered normal.

I'm perfectly happy to be labelled eccentric in such a world. Freud said that sanity could only be defined in relation to society as a whole. What if it's society that's crazy? Do we identify with it then, for the sake of appearances?

Perhaps when we're young the pressure to conform, to make our way in this mad world, is too strong to resist. Although there have always been drop-outs.

The tragedy today is that too many of our young are being forced out. Half the young people living rough on the streets would have been in art colleges in my time, not begging. Well done, Consumer Society, you sure know how to take care of your children.

Actually, my friend Marty has a very interesting theory about all that. He says it's no accident the Tribes of Israel were wandering in the desert for forty years. Anyone who's been there knows that with the worst navigator in the world it can't take more than a week or so to walk from Egypt to Israel. So what were they doing the rest of the time?

Well, consider. The people who came out of Egypt were soft, used to living in a slave situation. Forty years is what it takes for a new generation to grow to maturity. A hungry, aggressive generation, ripe for a bit of rape and pillage on the way to taking over a lot of other people's property.

Forty years was the period between the end of the Second World War and the Thatcher era. A lot of highly trained combat men came back from that war to a country ruled by a thousand year old aristocracy with a few unarmed policemen to protect them. Of course those returning servicemen had to be pandered to, else we might have had a real revolution on this island at last. But it didn't happen.

The children of those homecoming heroes were given everything their aristocratic forbears traditionally reserved for themselves, until, forty years later, we were so soft and spoiled, we accepted anything they did to us when it was time to take all the goodies away again. Makes you think, huh?

Incidentally, how come it's OK for the rich to have Nannies for their off-spring, but the Nanny state is supposed to be something to be reviled? Just wondering. . . .

Age should take the pressure off having to pretend we haven't noticed that the world is barmy. I'm old and outraged at what I see going on around me. I know I'm sane, cos my analyst told me so. But people get driven mad by living the lie that everything's hunky dory when their own senses tell them civilisation as we know it is falling apart.

Don't worry if what you choose to do with the last years of your life doesn't quite fit in with what your neighbours are up to. To all intents and purposes, this is the only life you've got. Make the most of it, whatever anybody else says. Seeing you having a ball can make lesser spirits jealous. Are you going to clip your wings to suit them? Or shake your tail as you fly off into a glorious sunset?

Crazy? Who's crazy? Not me, sister, that's for damn sure!

YES CHILDREN. WE FINALLY
GOT RID OF THE HIDEOUS
'NANNY' STATE, THAT
THROTTLED INCENTIVE AND
PERSONAL ACHIEVEMENT, THAT
TOOK AWAY OUR WILL TO
WIN AND MADE US LOSERS.
NOW I'M 'MORE, AND YOU
MAY CALL ME....

STEPMOTHER!

THORN

DISABLED DOESN'T MEAN YOU CAN'T

Once I walked, but not too far!
Couldn't wait til I owned a car!
Once I ran, but not too fast!
Over-exertion makes me gasp!

Now I sit or lie and dream,
Like a cat afloat in cream!
All I want is round my bed,
Or floating free inside my head.

But while I've still got half a lung,
I'll make sure I exercise my tongue!

When the vigour of youth is displaced by the restrictions of age, it's time to dig deep for a sense of humour. "There's nothing good or bad, but thinking makes it so", said the Bard of Avon. How true. You may not be able to do anything about your loss of mobility, but you can do something about your attitude.

Don't grumble because you need to be wheeled in a chair - thank your lucky stars you don't have to get worn out walking.

Need people to assist you? How great to have company!

Living in pain may be hell on earth, but you might as well assume you're paying off some karmic debt and get on with it as graciously as possible.

I just hope that when my time comes, I remember my own advice!

ROCK 'N' ROLL IS GOOD FOR THE SOUL

A hundred thousand children,
All playing in the sun,
Laughing, pretending
That life is only fun.

A hundred thousand children,
All rolling up the grass,
And here and there a skinhead,
Kicking arse.

And like a shadow across the moon,
The policemen call the tune,
Yes, like a shadow across the moon,
The party's over!

Don't they know that we're at war,
The rich are starving out the poor?
Doesn't anybody care,
Tomorrow may just not be there?

And like a shadow across the moon,
The policemen call the tune.
Yes, like a shadow across the moon,
The party's over!

I really try to play along,
To join in with their silly song,
But when I see the signs of death,
It sort of takes away my breath.

And like a shadow across the moon,
The policemen call the tune,
Yes, like a shadow across the moon,
The party's over!

Ever been to a rave? Or a festival? You should go. See for yourself what the kids are really up to, instead of believing the propaganda spewed out by the media.

Celebrating life was always part of our tribal heritage. They may not know it, but the kids are reaching back into atavistic roots when they trip out to the boom boom music.

Elders should be on hand, when they do that. And I don't mean as authority figures, but as guides, if we're needed. You'd feel safe somewhere like Glastonbury Festival, if you like camping. There's enough policemen there to put you off smoking dope for life. They permit it. Oh, how I hate being patronised! I went there recently. Wouldn't have missed it for the world - even if I did have to perform in a field!

Does us all the world of good, sleeping under the stars once in a while, touching the earth, tribal rythmns pounding through your dreams. . . . Mind you, as my friend Evie once advised me, it's good to take some sort of mattress with you. After a certain age, waking up on the hard earth just doesn't feel like a pleasure! More an assault course!

Never condemn what you haven't experienced yourself. Never believe half what you read in the papers. And yes, the music probably will be too loud to bear. But the vibrations. . .
. . . . . !

SAVE THE WORLD!

Where are the heroes
Who fought for the light?
Where are they sleeping
In the world's long night?
The children are hungry,
The animals are dead,
The rivers are dirty,
There are worms in the bread.
We can't look to others
To help us survive,
It's time that each human
Found their own inner drive.
Where are the heroes,
Be they ever so few.
Wake up, you deadheads,
The heroes are you!

One thing I've learned as I've got older, is that it helps to have a purpose in life.

I'm not the sort of person who can sit happily, doing nothing, letting life flow on around me. I admire people who can, but I think there's too much work to be done in today's world to ignore it all myself.

I think we're all here for a reason. We have lessons to learn, debts to pay and duties to perform. Getting old doesn't release us from those obligations. Rather it increases the urgency to get on and deal with whatever little bit it falls to our lot to take care of.

Wherever you are, however small your sphere of influence, by filling a space on the planet, you have a responsibility to do the best you can. Well, that's what I think.

The world doesn't owe me a living, but I owe the world everything. It feeds me, it gives me beautiful views, it offers me other life forms for companionship. If I can do anything to help save it from complete desecration, I will.

KNOW YOURSELF!

How come I'm supposed to be
Responsible for your sanity?
We're all born and die alone,
I've got enough trouble with my own!
So what, our parents couldn't cope,
Or drove us mad, or into dope?
It's still down to each of us
To handle our own psychic pus!
You may need help, so see a shrink!
It's not as bad as you might think.
I don't say you should take the pills,
There are ways of talking through our ills.
But if you think this world is s***,
Please look at your own part in it!

My friend Roger says that he's noticed that as you get older you learn to live in the moment more. It's what mystics and meditators have been working towards for years. And it's ours, by divine right of getting older. By keeping our wits about us.

Because that's the secret of a successful old age - an active brain. When you're alert, things happen. It's easy to slip into vegetable mode and become just another miserable old bugger cluttering up the scenery. Bad enough such a thing should happen to you through ill-health. Unforgivable if it's voluntary. But there are a lot of people about who think that life ends at thirty and everything after that will just be a grey waste of grumbling conformity.
Well, not if you're having a good time it won't.

Nobody's going to give it to you on a plate, however. It's up to each of us to make our own futures.

And we do have a future, individually and collectively. The world isn't going to end at a minute to midnight, December 31st. 1999. Survival may get tougher in the first decades of the 21st. century, civilisation as we know it may breakdown, but life will go on. It's in our hands what sort of life, however,whether we adapt and outwit the new order, or not.

Life is a creative process. I know it is. But we have to take responsibility for ourselves. "Oh God, Mother", my son's groaning, "The R word again!" Well, sorry, kid, but that's how it is.

The wisest maxim in the world is "Know Yourself". It's what was written over the doorway at Delphi, it was the object of the Eleusian Mysteries, it's what astrology is really about, it's what counsellors and analysts earn their money helping people do, it's what the confessional was originally designed for. Until we know ourselves, until we clear out those ghost voices from the past - you know the ones, they keep haunting us with what we ought to be doing, what we should be like, what's right and wrong according to so and so's definition - until we silence all that chatter we can't hear the still, small voice of our inner being, or our higher self, call it what you like. That's the voice us oldies should be responding to. Our own.

As we get older, our spiritual power gets stronger, our psychic powers flourish, our magickal powers escalate. If we don't take responsibility for the effect we have, we could be adding to the world's woes without even being aware of it. And ignorance is no defence in spiritual law, any more than it is in criminal law. So watch it!

I don't know if I've got one year left or twenty. Whichever it is, I plan to enjoy it. I may travel in my inner universe, or get out on the road. I may find a community to live among or stay on my own. I may even set up my own business. Who knows? Whatever I do, I'll be following my instinct and working for the light. That's the main thing.

And if I leave any footprints in the sand, on my way up the mountain, don't be afraid to follow me. If there's enough of us around up there we can all have a party!

Now that's what I call the way to go!

ONE LAST THING GIRLY, ALWAYS REMEMBER, NO MATTER HOW OLD, HOW ILL, HOW HURT NOTHING CAN TAKE AWAY THE FACT YOU ARE WOMAN, SHE! IT CAN'T BE STOLE BY NO-ONE, THE ONLY TIME ITS LOST IS IF YOU GIVE IT AWAY, CATCH BYE

A selection of other titles from Capall Bann:

Available through your local bookshop, or direct, post free in the UK, from Capall Bann at: Freshfields, Chieveley, Berks, RG16 8TF.

Celtic Lore & Druidic Ritual By Rhiannon Ryall

Inevitably the Druidic Path crosses that of any genuine Gaelic Tradition of Wicca, so this book contains much druidic lore. Background material on the Druids is included, explaining much of their way of viewing the world & enabling the reader to understand more fully their attributions in general & their rituals in particular. The book is divided into five parts: 1: Casting circles, seasonal sigils, wands, woods for times of the year, Celtic runes, the Great Tides, making cones & vortices of power, polarities & how to change them, the seasonal Ogham keys & Ogham correspondences. 2: Old calendar festivals & associated evocations, the "Call of Nine", two versions of the 'Six Pointed Star Dance', Mistletoe Lore, New Moon working, the Fivefold Calendar. 3: Underlying fundamentals of magical work, magical squares, the Diamond Working Area. 4: Five initiations, including a shamanic one, some minor 'calls', some 'little magics'. 5: Background information on the Celtic path, the Arthurian myth & its underlying meaning & significance, the Three Worlds of the Celts, thoughts regarding the Hidden Path & final advice. ISBN 1 898307 225   £9.95

Auguries and Omens - The Magical Lore of Birds By Yvonne Aburrow

The folklore & mythology of birds is central to an understanding of the ancient world, yet it is a neglected topic. This book sets out to remedy this situation, examining in detail the interpretation of birds as auguries & omens, the mythology of birds (Roman, Greek, Celtic & Teutonic), the folklore & weather lore associated with them, their use in heraldry & falconry & their appearances in folk songs & poetry. The book examines these areas in a general way, then goes into specific details of individual birds from the albatross to the yellowhammer, including many indigenous British species, as well as more exotic & even mythical birds. ISBN 1 898307 11 3   £10.95

Crystal Clear - A Guide to Quartz Crystal By Jennifer Dent

This book answers the need for a basic and concise guide to quartz crystal - solving the many confusions and contradictions that exist about this fascinating topic, without being too esoteric or straying too far from the point. Crystals particularly clear quartz crystals, evoke a response, which can not be rationally explained; they inspire a sense of the sacred, of mystery, magic and light. This book explores why crystals are important, their place in history, cleansing, clearing, charging, energising/programming your crystals and techniques for using them for healing. Also included is a chapter on the formation & scientific aspects of quartz which is written in a humourous style to help offset the generally mind-numbing effects of talking physics with non-physicists. Jennifer has worked with crystals for many years, using them for healing & other purposes. ISBN 1 898307 30 X   £7.95

The Enchanted Forest - The Magical Lore of Trees By Yvonne Aburrow

This is a truly unique book covering the mythology, folklore, medicinal & craft uses of trees. Associated rhymes & songs are also included together with the esoteric correspondences - polarity, planet, deity, rune & Ogham. There is a short history of tree lore, its purpose & applications. A further section gives information on tree spirits & their importance. The text is profusely illustrated with line drawings by the author & artist Gill Bent. This book will appeal to anyone who likes trees.
ISBN   1-898307-08-3   £10.95

The Sacred Ring - The Pagan Origins of British Folk Festivals & Customs
By Michael Howard

From Yuletide to Hallowe'en, the progress of the year is marked in folk tradition by customs & festivals, recording the changing seasons. Some events are nominally Christian because the early church adopted many of the practices & beliefs of the pagan religions to supplant them. All over Europe, including Britain, seasonal customs & folk rituals dating from the earliest times are still celebrated. Some festivals belong to a seasonal pattern of the agricultural cycle, others record the mystical journey of the Sun across the sky, both dating back to pagan religions. Each is a unique happening combining Pagan & Christian symbolism to create seasonal celebrations which can be experienced on many different levels of understanding & enjoyment.

The old festivals & folk customs which are still celebrated all over the British Isles each year represent a survival of the ancient concept of a seasonal cycle based on the sacredness of the land & the earth. The Sacred Ring of the year is a reminder of our ancient past & is still a potent symbol for the 20th century. It reminds us of humankind's integral link with Nature, even in our modern technological society, which is reflected in the ritual pattern of the changing seasons of the ecological cycle. ISBN 1 898307 28 8   £9.95

In Search of Herne the Hunter   By Eric L. Fitch

The book commences with an introduction to Herne's story & his relationship with Windsor, the oak on which Herne hanged himself & its significance in history & mythology. The next section investigates antlers & their symbology in prehistoric religions, together with a study of the horned god Cernunnos, the Wild Hunt & its associations with Woden, Herne etc. & the Christian devil. There is a descriptive chapter on the tradition of dressing up as animals & the wearing & use of antlers in particular. Herne's suicide & its connection with Woden & prehistoric sacrifice is covered, together with the most complete collection of Herne's appearances, plus an investigation into the nature of his hauntings. Photographs, illustrations & diagrams enhance the authoritative & well researched text. The book also contains appendices covering the 19th century opera on the legend of Herne, Herne & his status in certain esoteric circles & Herne & Paganism/Wicca.   ISBN 1 898307 237   Price £9.95

Angels & Goddesses - Celtic Paganism & Christianity
by Michael Howard

This book traces the history and development of Celtic Paganism and Celtic Christianity specifically in Wales, but also in relation to the rest of the British Isles including Ireland, during the period from the Iron Age, through to the present day. It also studies the transition between the old pagan religions & Christianity & how the early Church, especially in the Celtic counmtries, both struggled with & later absorbed the earlier forms of spirituality it encountered. The book also deals with the way in which the Roman Catholic version of Christianity arrived in south-east England & the end of the 6th century, when the Pope sent St. Augustine on his famous mission to convert the pagan Saxons, & how this affected the Celtic Church.. It discusses how the Roman Church suppressed Celtic Christianity & the effect this was to have on the history & theology of the Church during the later Middle Ages. The influence of Celtic Chhristianity on the Arthurian legends & the Grail romances is explored as well as surviving traditions of Celtic bardism in the medieval period.

The conclusion on the book covers the interest in Celtic Christianity today & how, despite attempts to eradicate it from the pages of clerical history, its ideas & ideals have managed to survive & are now influencing New Age concepts & are relevent to the critical debate about the future of the modern chrurch. ISBN 1-898307-03-2 £9.95

The Magical Lore of Herbs by Marion Davies

There are plenty of herbals around, but none like this This marvellous book concentrates on the magical properties, folklore, history & craft of herbs together with their medicinal uses where applicable. Why & how herbs are used, their mythical associations & symbolism, all are detailed within these pages. The use of herbs has long been associated with paganism & the Old Religion, this book provides a wealth of information not only for modern day pagans, but for everyone interested in this fascinating topic. Marion Davies has an immense practical knowledge of herbs & their uses in treating humans & animals in addition to their more esoteric applications. This knowledge, coupled with her highly readable writing style makes this a must for anyone interested in herblore. The detailed researched text is well illustrated with line drawings. ISBN 1 898307 14 8   £10.95

The Lore of the Sacred Horse - The Magical Lore of Horses By Marion Davies

Man's debt to the horse (and it's relatives) is immeasurable. For thousands of years before recorded history, man pushed forward his civilisations and conquests on the back of a horse and viewed his domains between a horse's ears. Man and horse are inextricably woven together into a relationship which is without equal in the rest of creation. Even Man's 'best friend', the dog, cannot claim the impact of the horse. This noble animal has been food and transport, the innocent participant in Man's wars, at one time his Deity and the honoured companion of his Deities. The symbol of majesty and power. From seed-time to harvest, the horse has been at the forefront of agricultural economy. Even so, Man's faithful servant has known the full extent of cruelty and ingratitude, may the Gods forgive us. The past fifty years have seen a dramatic increase in the popularity of the horse in our leisure pursuits and it once more takes it's rightful place - that of Man's companion.

This book traces this relationship from earliest times, stressing the religio-magical aspects. The Sacred Horse is rooted deep within our race-memory and is still to be found in our high-tech culture. ISBN 1 898307 19 9 £10.95

Pathworking 2nd Ed. By Pete Jennings & Pete Sawyer

A pathworking is a guided meditational exercise, used for many different aims, from raising consciousness to healing rituals. No particular beliefs or large sums of money are needed to benefit from it & it can be conducted within a group or solo at time intervals to suit you. Learn how to alter your conscious state, deal with stress, search for esoteric knowledge or simply have fun & relax. It starts with a clear explanation of the theory of pathworking and shows in simple & concise terms what it is about and how to achieve results, then goes on to more advanced paths & how to develop your own, it also contains over 30 detailed and explained pathworkings. Highly practical advice & information is given on how to establish and manage your own group. ISBN 1 898307 00 8 £7.95

Living Tarot By Ann Walker

A simple guide to the Tarot, for both divination and discovery of the inner self requiring no previous knowledge. This book commences with background information on how the Tarot works and a brief history of the origins of these fascinating cards. To get the best out of the Tarot, it is necessary to have both an intuitive understanding of the cards and a working knowledge of the basic understanding of their meanings. Ann passes on her knowledge and thoughts gained in over 20 years practical experience using and teaching the Tarot. She concentrates on practical information put forward in an easy to read, no nonsense style.

The book includes a number of layouts for the Tarot, from simple layouts for the beginner to more complex spreads for the more experienced practitioner. Also included are details on astrological connections with the Tarot and the use of the cards as aids to meditation. The text is well illustrated, making the information easy to follow and apply. ISBN 1 898307 27 X   £7.95